HORSE TRACKS

HORSE TRACKS

poems

Henry Real Bird

LOST HORSE PRESS
Sandpoint, Idaho

ACKNOWLEDGMENTS

Before we get started I want to thank Corby Skinner and Laila Nelson of *Writer's Voice* for believing in me when I was alone standing out in the hills. Hal Cannon, the crew in Elko, and my many friends have kept me alive and I just want to say, *thank you,* for helping with the kind words. The people who caused me to write the way I do, thank you for being. My family is the reason that I am here, so I am thankful for them.

FIRST EDITION

Senior Editor: Christi Kramer
Cover Art by Chuck DeHaan: "WaterBreaking"
  Other fine Western paintings by C. DeHaan can be viewed online at
  www.chuckdehaan.com.
Author Photo by Joseph Terry
Book Design by Christine Holbert

CATALOGUING-IN-PUBLICATION DATA

Real Bird, Henry.
  Horse tracks : poems / Henry Real Bird.—1st ed.
    p. cm.
  ISBN 978-0-9844510-5-0 (alk. paper)
  I. Title.
  PS3568.E255H67 2010
  811'.54—dc22
                        2010039008

TABLE OF CONTENTS

II. Reflections & Shadows

III. *Place Setting for a Feast of People No Longer Here*

enry Real Bird breaks a lot of the rules my formal education taught me about writing poetry, but half of Henry's education comes from somewhere else. When Crow is your primary language and your poetry is Crow spoken in English, the rules most likely get written as you go.

If you have had the opportunity to hear Henry, you realize that he has found inspiration for his written work while riding his Big Lodge Clan's history up Yellow Leggins Creek and looking out at the Wolf Teeth range.

It is one thing to see the influence of the cowboy myth and of country-western music in Henry's work. It is quite another to realize that he was born into the life and language of the Plains Indian horse culture. He can be "the cowboy working the gate to the stockyards bound semi," or he can be the Indian shaking the "buffalo bull testicle-covered rattle." Either way, he combs "the mane of a pony sort of insane." Henry's poetry can at one moment show the sentiments of the American Romantic tradition and at the next go for the brutal honesty the reality his marginalized existence has required: "If it gets worse, I can always kill myself."

Leslie Fiedler writes at the end of *The Montana Face*, "... so long as the Montanan fails to come to terms with the Indian, despised and outcast in his open-air ghettos, just so long will he be incapable of coming to terms with his own real past, of making the adjustment between myth and reality upon which a successful culture depends."

Hank Real Bird had no choice in making that adjustment, but the good Crow Montanan that he is, he has done it well, in his life and in his poetry—for all of us.

—*Greg Keeler*

I

Beyond Reflection

Love is a lasting moment,
A robin in winter sky

BEYOND REFLECTION

Where the soul lives in the mind of some who know not only the body, I go riding through, whipping over and under in the beautiful colors of the morning sun. I curry my thoughts. Out here in the hills, the soul of the poet lies in his work. Life is made of hills and mountains. You climb to the top of a hill or a mountain, and yet, there is another to climb. Up and down these draws, coulees and rivers, my people followed the buffalo on a horse economy in their quest for food.

Where it is high—buttes and mountain tops—my people would come to ask for good things from He Who First Did Everything. Thoughts, feelings and life, they would ask for in the wind that is good from where it is high. "The wind, in it, what is good there is a lot, they say. Days that are good, a lot may you use with your heart good, your thoughts good. With no illness, may you go winters many to get enough of who you love. Wind that is good may you use. Your story, may it be good. These, I have asked for you," said my Grandfather Owns Painted Horse one time just before the sun came out. Today it was beautiful as the sunshine hit the snow-covered tops of the Wolf Teeth Mountains.

If your heart is good playing your role
That is all we ask for in life's stroll.

The thoughts are in, so let us go saddle up a thought, and ride it around in life as it is today. It is good that you have come; tomorrow, may you be lucky to have what you want.

1

ITCHIK

Beyond reflection, deep into a feeling,
Dreamt the sun appeared and before me mirrored,
In the circle sun glare was an eagle in the air,
Pure white eagle with wings spread out
Tail feathers seemed so thin in the sunlight.
Then into a bald eagle he turned
As he swooped into his flight
To go beyond reflection
And deep into a shadow of thought.
Among the stars, in a feeling.
The hills are pink
The sky is lavender.
I can feel your skin.
I hear your laughter.
Ponder.
As time went on, I began to think,
Thank you for being,
Listen, listen to this feeling
Suppressed by a society.
Just for love I wanted to hold you
In the balance of life.
I wish I were a Big Lodge Crow Indian warrior
Who could swoop up a beautiful Piegan woman
Going after water, but I have to ponder.
Love to me is a feeling,
A feeling of life in love.

The breath-giving kiss in the morning mist
The art of loving is enticed by a beautiful feeling.
Want you to feel beautiful.
In the heat of the day,
Come and take me away

To the mouth of Medicine Tail Coulee.
From the Little Big Horn River,
Water will you give me,
From beyond reflection, into your feeling?
The birds have gone
And the leaves have turned yellow.
First snow has reached us,
Sheep Mountain is white with it.
A few nights ago through the teepee's neck
The moon, she peeked in to give me moon shadow
In front of my fire shadow.
So blessed was I to meet my shadows,
I'm lucky, I know.
The first rays of the sun
Touched the tip of Wolf Teeth
In a day of love and fun.
To you, my dream,
I shall love you forever
From the feeling who's deep within.
Snug within stirrups of wood
Where within I stood
With a heart that's good.
The best of what is good
Is to trot upon a ridge
In the spring after the rains,
In thoughts of love as I even my reins.
Where the daytime star is next to crescent moon,
For the buffalo young are, as life arrived,
Under sunburst blanket of love.
I fell beyond reflection, deep into a feeling.
Itchik hilauka!
Good it is now!
The sun is about to appear
And upon a ridge
I'm trotting along.

This is where I belong
In the spring after the rains
When the grass is deep.
My heart is so good at this time
In the spring, again in the fall
When I'm trotting along,
Trotting along upon a ridge.
This is the best of what is good
From within my stirrups of wood
Where within I stood
To think thoughts of love for you.
Beyond reflection, deep into your feeling,
As I'm trotting along upon a ridge
In the spring after the rains
When the grass is deep.
My heart is good at this time.

Over the hill is another feeling, it seems. Yes, over the hill
There is good grass, good water for I saw coyote tracks
Headed over the hill. Over the hill and into tomorrow.
I know only what I know.
Before, how it used to be
It will never be, that I know.
But when that grass appears
Grass that is green, I smell,
And you I would like to see.
Cannot invest my feelings,
Kept ringing and ringing in my mind
As I lie awake on Yellow Leggings Creek,
Tears flow in my heart
To drown the emptiness.
A bronc can have a bad trip
When the stakes are high.
No need to beg for love
When it passes you by.
My innermost is comatose.
All I wanted was to kiss you lightly
In the middle of the night
To tell you that I love you.
But anyway I wish you love
In a world of now shadows
Life in glaring vacuum.
Let me check for your bill of sale.

Dance if you will,
But when did I walk out
On this transparent plain?
Hey, when you're dancing to the music,
It's yours.

You, yourself, will know when to stop.
I know only what I know.
Before, how it used to be
It will never be, that I know.
But when that grass appears,
Grass that is green, I smell
And you I would like to see.

As the forms and shapes
Begin to emerge
The many colors and shades
Of day and night merge.
Spurs jingle to rope corral
Hoof beats thunder in steady trot
Out among stars, a feeling fell,
And within you I sought.
I remembered eating wild rosebud petals
Out among the Wolf Teeth Mountains
Feeling your love as it settles
A paint horse breaks and runs.

Leaves, the wind inside, they fly.
Leaves, the water within, they go.
Feeling, the wind among, they lie.

So I think
I'm taking my tack
On over to Medicine Bow
From the end of the slack

To disappear into a misty low.
The overhead fling,
The cowboy never asks for a horse
And not much sweat for the way he rode
As he keeps on riding.

Leaves, the wind inside, they fly.
Leaves, the water within, they go.
Feeling, the wind among, they lie.

REFLECTION

On a moonlit night
Out in the hills
I gazed into the many stars
As a low mist lightly whispered
A feeling, pink twilight conceals,
In yellow orange red maroon
Beautiful colors round river's tip.
Pine tree-lined horizon
Captured in a silvery moon
Was a feeling alongside the road.
But I'm riding circle,
Remembering a feeling, alongside the road.

Need to bathe
In the moonlight
At the river's tip
In fall colors.
I felt the cold wind last night
So I reached into the moon's reflection
On the Little Big Horn
And asked for your love.
Pine tree-lined horizon
Captured in a silvery moon
Was a feeling alongside the road
But I'm riding circle,
Remembering a feeling, alongside the road.

BUFFALO GRASS

Buffalo grass story, the greasy grass
From the Big Horn Mountains
Comes a chestnut bronc named Coke High.
Bells he's rung for some who try.
At one time, this bronc twister
Was awarded a re-ride.
Coke High was a chute-fighting
Board-busting outlaw in the re-ride draw
That chased this twister away,
Who now cuts the hay from CRP land.
The buffalo grass flicks as sun turns
To go into another winter nick.
From an ancient Crow Indian lookout
I think of life, think of those
Who have gone through
This beautiful and luscious buffalo grass.
Billy the Kid, Battle of the Little Big Horn,
Johnson County Range Wars, over the buffalo grass.
But why not bid, I've always sworn,
Supply and demand in books and jars.
Landless peoples' land
Mountain range unit grazing fees
To more than double,
$1.86 to $4.28, they tease.
Night Horse in a bubble,
Man's best friend eats
On about $10 a moon
But a sell-out Indian
Can get $12.50 AUM
For non-Indian cow/calf pair
On buffalo grass on the Big Horn.
What is so different about Crow Indian land?

Mother Earth sold for $1.50 an acre, I'm told.
In another state of mind
They talk of meritocracy
At crust of xenophobia
For the mental mediocrity
In waltzing journey to utopia.
Heart that is strong is it,
Ole Tex could do most of it
But was too small for King Ranch,
Took command from willow branch.
The Texas Twister Zettle
Subsidies he never meddles
Because the cowboy
Alone represented toughness, rugged individualism,
To live with the mystic Indian.
My heart is bad (no good)
Because the farmer thinks he's a cowboy
And the Indian thinks he's Anglo
In a cultural mirage.

A COTTONWOOD LEAF

To see the firstborn
Of a longhorn heifer with one horn
As she gives her protection
Is a feeling of great satisfaction.
Baby calves bucking
Give me this feeling
But when the wind hits you in the face,
Think of me.
This brown cottonwood leaf
Floated down the muddy waters
Of Mean River.
I'm that feeling that never was
But just a reminder of yester-winter
In a mind that never was
The feeling dissipated
In relation to the premise
That feelings never leave
Or they never were
To be thought of in sleepless nights
Of what is
To an individual alone
That never was.
This brown cottonwood leaf
Floated down the muddy waters
Of Mean River.
I'm that feeling that never was
But just a reminder of yester-winter
In a mind that never was
The feeling dissipated

SEMANTICS

Never ending flow of talk
Evasive babble crumpling
And flowing downstream
Just a democratic washout
That we talk about every ten years.
The trade off in change
On the electric horseman's range
It's not the system
That is bad
It's the people in it,
My dear lad.
Give and take written on the wall,
But will you call
With a hypocritical mind
And a money heart?
In the monetary ecosystem
You probably comprise a kissing committee.
"I'm not creative.
I just follow and describe
The four different grounds we go through
As the faces change
And feelings come and go.
"I've got understanding,
The security of bewilderment in confidence,"
Said a ghost at a wishing well.
In the turbulence of legal tender,
The Indian washes up
On the beach of poverty.
Life never ends
It just changes form,
Wal-Mart is the buffalo.
Semantics?

Give and take written on the wall,
But will you call
With a hypocritical mind
And a money heart?
In the monetary ecosystem
You probably comprise a kissing committee.

THOUGHT

"Thought is like a cloud
You can see through shadow to see nothing
But you can see shadow
When it touches something you know,
Like that cloud's shadow
Touching the Wolf Teeth Mountains.
When the clouds touch the mountain's top
Or where it is high
The wind is good
When you're among the clouds
Blurred ground among fog,
You are close to He Who First Did Everything,"
Said my Grandfather Owns Painted Horse.
We are but nomads asking for nothing
But the blessings upon our Mother Earth.
We are born as someone new
So then
We have to be taught
The good from the bad.
What is good, we want you to know.
What is good, we want you to use,
In the way that you are a person.

Wanted to open your dreams
To look within
The twinkle in your eyes
On blessed wishful thoughts.
The Chinook winds roared on
Somewhere down Yellow Leggings
In the bitter sting of winter cold.
A very old story is told
By the people of before
Way down in my vein's core
Flow thoughts of wolf's lore.
A kiss is a feeling in trust
In the beginning way before lust.
Little children of the Large Beaked Bird
Were sent in wolf den.
There's a place out there
Where the she-wolf touches the child
With the moist tip of her nose,
The bond of coexistence
From the darkness in Mother Earth.
The child brings out
Wolf pups before they can see
To live outside the teepee
To warn of something in the night
And to carry the load by day.

Under a purple lavender
Dappled orange sky,
Remembered a story of laughter
When I heard wolf howl cry
On Yellow Leggings in Wolf Teeth,
Out there the Big Dipper beneath.

In the moon we passed
When little currents
With little babbles
Move under melting snow
On down from the river's tip
To break the ice on Greasy Grass.
The return of the geese
On a skiff of snow
Over the green grass ground appearing,
The moon slid into a reddish blue sky
In the land of men's cloud.
The Indian and wolf followed the buffalo
On land of good grass and water.
"Here, meat that is good
I feed to you.
Meat that is good, bring for me,"
A child of the Large Beaked Bird would say
As he fed the wolf dog.

Under a purple lavender
Dappled orange sky
Remembered a story of laughter
When I heard wolf howl cry
On Yellow Leggings in Wolf Teeth,
Out there the Big Dipper beneath.

Can't really do much of anything
As salty sweat stains hardened on my pony,
Seems as if a big heavy rain
And light hail dropped on us.
The soaked terrain
Illuminated a pale-colored surface
Of ash stained lavender bluish layers.
Mother Earth cupped her hand
For the cowboy to ride through
The twilight in the breaks land.
A growing attitude,
The rhythm has to go where you want
Not where it may.
But until my memories go blind,
Why rope,
If you're not going to ride?
Why run the horses in
If you're not going to ride?
But may the horses return.
Odd numbered geese
Over Wolf Teeth
Cast feeling beneath.
My soul has gone east
To leave me sleepless.
The death of a feeling,
In the sunlight through the teepee's neck
The fine dust ascends gently.
Sparkling in the sunlight
Are my feelings.
For love stood still, alive in her tracks
In the sunlight to ascend gently
Through the teepee's neck.

GHOSTLY THOUGHT

"In the silence of the hills
I dreamt of a feeling," said this ghost,
"To know that I'll never have love
Enters my mind from time to time
But I close my eyes,
To glide on the ice.
Drifting back into fantasy
For I don't exist in reality,
But in reality I can smell your sweetness.
You got me to write again.
This emptiness, a void, a hole in the sky
Is where I go out of my life
Spinning round in no rhyme.
I'll get the rhythm back in rhyme.
Just a feeling, a taste of love,
Hold tight, glimpse disappearing of dew.
Good morning, wish I could see me
In your beauty in the morning
With the star that is light.
Try to make me feel right,
That's the way
I'd like to see me in your beauty,
Swirling in the beautiful colors
Before the coming of the sun
In the silence of the hills
I dreamt of a feeling."

Bird Horse
Next to the star that is light,
In child's play, unaware,
Some people live in caverns of their minds
To never hear talk before the treaties
Trickling down the veins.
Crumbled eye tooth thought
Which lives between the grass and stars
Trickling down the veins.
To say
Some Crows are riding upside down
And falling into money
Where the aborted live
In the policies of the Bureau of Indian Affairs.
That's why the Maker showed the water beings
At the edge of the Big Horn Mountains
As the long otter lives on in white clouds
Trickling down the veins
Next to the star that is light.
Bird Horse
A sovereign on the plains
In knee high buffalo grass
Next to the star that is light.

NIGHT AND DAY

She taught me to talk in prayer, in Sun Dance,
To be connected with Mother Earth
To love again in rebirth.
I bit the sagebrush
As the eagle claw pierced into my chest
Beyond the pain, prayers mixed with tears.
You were the best,
To stay alive in feelings for years
But then again, you were perfection.
Beauty of sound blew in our feelings,
Love returned affection.
My skin broke
And I was free in your love,
That was perfection in your arms.
At that very moment in time
I knew then that I was blessed.
But there are times when I can't wait,
I'm thankful for the wide open spaces
As I ride out on buffalo trails and cow trails
Where wolves have gone.
As I ride out into the wide open spaces
Where a cloud and her shadow
Are the main characters
Lost somewhere deep in my memories,
Night is with day.

Ice-backed, powder-snow-dusted longhorn cattle
Moving slowly in cold, dust-snowy morning
As I ride alone in your feeling.
I've been listening to the silence
Out among the Wolf Teeth.
You've touched my heart like the silent burst
Of shooting stars descending homeward
To our Mother Earth.
This morning I saw the horizon stretch
Over in the country where the Black Lodge hunt,
The spirit appeared to sun.
Just between you and me
I go dreaming beyond doubt, deep into a feeling.
The heathen Indian before beyond,
But past the reflection
Of a life he never knew.
After riding through the memories
In the nothingness of stories
Am I to exist merely as a question?
Your feelings resist, looking into a constellation
I forgot your memory last night.
Wolf pups frolicking in tall buffalo grass
But what is the connection?
Winds across the prairie blew
As the maggot tidies with his bite
From there commencing past the rot
Of a buffalo skull pure white?
The Indian licking institutional window glass
Of a life in fermentation.
Upon walking on
To the decomposed carcass of an Indian
Exhumed by the synthetic thrills and highs

Past the cold edges of oblivion
I know his soul still lies in the silent subconscious
Of a swindling, corrupt corporate lawyer
Walking down Fourteenth and K.
And yet there is another Indian
Sitting on the guard rail,
High flying feeling where I could hear
The beautiful voice of the woman in the drum,
The spirit of love.
A kindly thunderous cloud snapping and cracking lightning
Way high in the light wind
Thunder and lightning, sunlight in the rain.
Just a-riding along
Looking at my long shadow on the ground
Just a-riding along
On up to the backwaters, to the still waters
Where the wind whistles on over the water
To show me the sacredness of life
As I begin to speak on behalf
Of the wind, water and our Mother Earth.
The so-called primitive environmentalist
Softened his Mother's heart
When his tears touched the ground,
And with his flesh-offering held high,
He began to speak with He Who First Did Everything,
"This earth, our Mother, watch her always."
The grass has reached its fullest length
And the sun is two fists high,
Within the clouds in the sun
Emerged a buffalo for strength
In the thunder and lightning of the sky
Blessed in thoughts for the sunshine in the rain
May you safely reach the spring rain
With visions of horses, and in my dream
This Spirit Being said,

"The horses have returned."
That is what I have asked for you,
That may you use,
And winters many may you see.
In my dream the horses came down Medicine Tail
And crossed the Little Big Horn River
On their home trail,
On our Sacred Mother Earth.

RAMBLIN'

Ramblin' somewhere deep in memories
There is a day that I remember
I went to Mean River
To look for ghost writings
On dead trees, under the bark.
Written on the tree
Are the ghost writings,
Sometimes written on driftwood.
Out here in these supernatural feelings
The surrealist nomad
Skimmed a flat rock over water.
Make me love you,
He thought to say,
But as he looked away
The feeling disappeared.

From a hungry shoe
Licking candy wrappers
I come to you
Speaking of these matters.
The epitome existence
Of the Crow Indian eunuchs
In the corridors of the Bureau of Indian Affairs
Tinsel town thirst, federal credit union financed,
Tail between leg behavior,
Their ignorance enhanced
From Crow life they sever.
Indian rights for sale, broker BIA,
A person de-pantsed
Crow Indian baptism
But what did the psychiatrist say?
"One bird is worth two in the bush.
It's a man's walk,
You can't squeeze blood out of a board
And don't you forget it,"
Said the realist meadowlark
At the Prairie Chicken Dance.

COSMIC BEAUTY

In the dusk
Off toward where the sun comes out
Were some pink-capped thunderheads.
There was, once, a nice looking beauty
Woman of the Peigan . . . Clan of the Crow
All decked out and wrapped in buffalo robe
Decorated in the finest work of quill
With the many points of the sun upon her back.
I lift the teepee door to look inside
And there she was on a thick bed of cattails,
This cosmic beauty with light auburn hair
Necklace of crystal twinkling shining rock.
The fire burned gently by her side
And into her feeling I wanted to slide.
The dream comes first
From thoughts they burst,
Feeling in heart immersed
The starry-eyed curse.
Star Shine Wolf Child, spill me a feeling,
Splash on hide the beautiful longhorn galosh,
Red-scarfed cowboy moving about.
Know that you're successful
But what's to lose?
Just let me hold you
In idle sea
But to leave on the dew
To say you, I would like to see
Rhyme scheming around.
Love is a feeling in the wind
The colors of life, heart within thought
Beyond the talk blowing around

The spirit of life, the soul of man
Heart within thought beyond the talk,
Blowing around and around
Toward the bond of love
Between a man and a woman
Walking through rigors
Forever is a night alone in eternity
Happened so fast, wanted it to last
It was in the fall, I was in timber tall
When I saw this crystal dragonfly
In first frost before sun dew
Got this feeling that I want to live
Lord, it's something I can't explain
You've got me started before the sun dew
You've got this feeling that I was looking for,
Life's feeling in love
That was what I couldn't explain.
Remembered writing for you in the winters we've passed
The light warm winter breeze
Blew ripples over a puddle on Yellow Leggings
In the Wolf Teeth Mountains.
What if . . . if you ever think
Wolf Teeth Mountains I'll be among
For just a smile my heart was good,
The first warmth of summer heat
Checking for calves in warm Chinook winter winds
That came down Deernose Ridge to hit me in the face.
Longhorns calving
Ole' bay on mud slide,
Reckon that's the reason O-W on his hide.
You look fine teasing for just a smile,
My heart was good.
I would like to be on your mind
And to live in your fantasies,

I know you'll never be mine
But just to be in those capacities
As a feeling in the wind,
She took the scribblings.

In this moon of beautiful feelings
When the plum blossoms
Glitter beautiful fragrance
In the heart and bosom
In this moon
And for winters many to come,
Let love live in this lodge.
Never say never forever again
With nothing behind me, before, beyond
On a road that never ends
Life leaves me hoping for love.
Wishing my thumb luck
I walk out into the horizon
For the magic she possesses
In feelings of florescence
Radiant kaleidoscope impression
Tie-dyed and heart inside I tuck.
Chokecherry leaves move,
Buffalo roam, winter ends,
Crow People migrate, moving on,
Moving on up Wind River,
In this moon of beautiful feelings
In this moon of beautiful feelings
When the plum blossoms
Glitter beautiful fragrance
In the heart and bosom
In this moon
And for winters many to come,
Let love live in this lodge.

NECKLACE

In the sunlight through the teepee's neck
The fine dust ascended gently,
Sprinkled in the sunlight are my feelings
For love stood still alive in her tracks.
Close your eyes and I'll put this necklace
Upon your neck,
From the rustling of the wind
In the fluttering of feathers
In the cooing of a dove
Comes to you a feeling brought out
By the elk wood wind whistle.
The majestic proud prancing elk
Sucked in his composure
To let out a winsome whistle
That peaked out, then faded into a memory
In the completion of a circle
Where the beginning is the end
The raspy deep wood wind whistle
Rattled and bubbled in a motorized rhythm
From among the willows
On the inside of the river's bend
The whistling sound was sent
Flanked by the babbling of the water
To bounce off the daytime star.
The message of need
From a feeling freed,
I want you to want me
In ecstasy, relieved smile
I want you to want me
In love's gentle hold
Turned loose among the stars
Is the feeling I want from you.

Think of me, when the wind
Hits you on the face,
A feeling to embrace.
At one time, a long time ago,
There was a young man
Of the Mountain People Band
Wanted to be loved
By a beauty of lineage Piegan.
He asked her for water
But her feeling wouldn't falter,
Off he went to go without food and water,
This beauty's love he prayed for
Until day four
Just at the time of perfect rhyme
Below the star that is light
Overlooking a canyon in the Shining Mountains.
Me, you love,
That is what I want,
With me,
I want you to lose yourself.
What do you think?
To the stars we'll reach
That is what I'm thinking.
What do you think?
That's how it is
As the elk began to speak
Under pink clouds
In a turquoise background sky,
Just before the birth of shadows
Under the star that is light,
The sun was not yet out.
"You, I've seen, you have suffered,
Water and food you have not used."
As the feelings in leaves fluttered
Where a little river bottom goes,

The bull elk stood in his realm
As the first rays of the sun
Twinkled the mountain's top.
"What you've asked for, I know,
And now, you I want to help
To get the feeling to come out of beauty,
That is what I'm going to give you.
Watch me, this is how it is done."
As he backed up to suck in his composure
He let out his long swirling whistle
That seemed to return
To bring in all the cow elk
From down the canyon.
"You see that?
Up canyon I will now point."
To let his whistle go
That drew out all the cow elk
From that direction.
It was he that they wanted to know,
He owned the feelings
Of their offerings
For a gift of his creation.
"That is how it is,"
Said the bull elk.
"When you get home, don't you roam,
Tell grandfather in the sweat lodge
Take cedar pouch, to tell of me,
And what I have given to you, to be me.
When you're out of the lodge, after you bathe,
Get on your belly for a drink.
There will be a stick bobbing
In the swift lavender top river
As the daytime star touches the water
With his reflection.
Get that stick for it is what you use

To make your elk wood wind whistle.
Point in her direction
For it is her affection
You will draw out.
There is yet more, I haven't told
But some other time."
This young man of the Mountain People Band
Used his elk wood wind whistle
In the willows the whistle was sent,
The warrior's deeds in song,
Wood wind whistle tune
To draw out a feeling in you born,
The beauty of lineage Piegan
Followed the whistling sound
And wanted to be found.
She reached him
To throw her arms around him lightly
As the elk wood wind whistle
Floated in the light wind.
The young man quit
To turn her loose and walked away
To the circle of lodges
To begin his life
As he faded into a memory
At the completion of a circle
Where the beginning is the end.
The woman hexer was given,
From their lives were driven
To follow the beauty of a feeling
They can't explain
In the rasp deep sound
Of the elk wood wind whistle.
Free love and love to all
Till the day he's no longer tall,
But somewhere

Beyond the starlight of your mind
Will be the beauty of a feeling
In the raspy deep sound
The elk wood wind whistle
Will play on and on.
Here's an elk tooth necklace
For you my lady,
A feeling for your beauty.
As he stares into a barren arid land,
The cowboy turned to say
Let me waken you
Before the sun with a gentle kiss,
For from your mouth's water
Is the dew of love,
At your mouth's edge
Is where I will get
Your love for me,
As I water your feelings
With fresh sparkling words.
The cowboy
Faded into a memory
But took sleep in his saddlebag
To talk about nothing,
Building fences and weaning calves,
Getting ready for winter.
The cowboy sits alone
Out in the hills
Listening to the radio
Remembering days
When there was no glue
On the Durham cigarette papers
But now, Bull Durham
Is no longer made
For men working spade?

DISTANT THOUGHT

He walked out on his feelings—
Have you ever thought,
That there'd be yet another feeling?
Another feeling besides the one you already wear.
On a silent distant thought
I go over the Shining Mountains.
Pastel colors emerge into twilight
Of pink and blue hues
As feeling from heart spews.
When the color of the sky
Touches the still lake water,
Another day, a feeling passes by.

On a silent distant thought
He walks out on a prayer
In the sacredness of life.
A dream was told for Red Scarf
By Sings In The Wind.
In this dream it was summer
And at the river's edge
The grass was green
And the cottonwood shade was like dark.
Then there appeared a yellow weasel
Who was bucking, dancing, frolicking around.
That day, may Red Scarf reach
Along with his people
The feeling of perfection,
Where every breath is blessed.

MOON SCENT

Moon sent a feeling ricocheting from my heart,
From my heart a moon-scented feeling beams
And into a trance filled with beautiful dreams
Of love, hope, care, sharing in a heart that is good.
I awake into the rainbow on the mist of a good mood,
That is all I wanted as steam blows out the nostrils
Of my paint going up the grade front of jingling rowels.
Reality sets in the jagged pine, ceramic horse-dotted horizon
That has always been told in horse track puddle reflection.

Just in case I do not see the sunrise
Or if I die before I am done living
I just wanted to tell you that I love you.

Out here riding through the pines
That whisper feelings past times
Only the dry rosebud's hard red color dot
The winter to remind one of love's plot
To stand on top of Wolf Teeth to see the Big Horn blessings
You will never understand unless you drink of its water rings,
Wonder if your reflection is you for that reason
    I'm thinking of you
As I'm riding out to check on the horses in the dew.

Just in case I do not see the sunrise
Or if I die before I am done living
I just wanted to tell you that I love you.

STATIC INFORMATION

Riding out into the horizon to never arrive
As it is in the immediate future, but strive
Long range over the hill, squirrel gathers nuts
Inevitable good or bad, we've reached today's ruts
The rainbow is on this side of the horizon
Where the horses are grazing quietly in Cook Stove Basin.
Dogmatic devotion brain washing of man's peaceful
   flow in currency
Is the sadness of a drunken chief in sanity's truancy.
We go on living producing crank, pot, booze, offspring
Honesty and integrity in the silence ring,
In the absence of man out in the hills
Corruption taunts my tribesmen with tribal seals.
They've sold their souls for a piece of fat bacon
Non-Indian committee plans Indian fate forsaken
But deaf to Crow dollar-sign eyes.
First rays of sun whirls with hope flies
In my heart the message in fluorescent black lights
I ride along the side of paranoia waved rights,
Riding out into the horizon to never arrive,
Malfunction conjunction's ignition stuck and in gear
Corruption reflects motion in loud cheer.
Crow Nation creed-fattened steers
As starlight truths in sunshine veers
Homeward we all have a place to be
Snow-covered tracks and grass began to grow free
After a fictitious election
Hailstorm monetary inhalation.

ROBIN

Lost to a memory
In a sky of dreams
Where a kiss was temporary,
This feeling beams
A scent of life
In light golden yellow frost;
The bittersweet cold
Tinkling where rivers go,
A drifter
Floating through time
Where memories live
In early winter moon
The crystal dragonfly is
Alive in a moment,
Just wanted to know
That tomorrow was there,
In past future perfect feeling.
Love is a lasting moment,
A robin in winter sky.

My mother, I held her hand
When she was in pain,
Then among the stars I stand
On such a young winter night,
The moon of the first snow
Brought the cry from low
Where death is trying to bite.
Last breath was a strain
To release her free into happiness,
But our fires put the sadness
Upon our faces lit in darkness.
All of us, we know each other,
Moons have passed, but still bother
With the missing who gave me life.

IN THE WIND

There are a lot of nice things in the wind, they say,
The wind can move shadows around in the day
But in this moon, it has taken the water away,
Some little rivers up the Little Big Horn are going dry
And today I heard the Musselshell went dry,
The wind has kept the clouds at bay
While the horses' hooves are dry to stay
Even though the Medicine Man sees no rain in the moon
He continues to ask for fall rains in his ceremony
To water Mother Earth to sing her tune,
The water can move shadows around in the day
In much the same movement feelings sway,
All I am asking for is just a feeling, if you can spare
As I've seen your beauty fixed in my stare
And with my feelings of love I want to share
With you the exquisitely radiant glow of my heart.

I can hear the waters of the Little Big Horn
As they swiftly babble clear from the mountain
Untouched, your heart was there born
A feeling chasing butterflies in flower fragrance abundant
In the time of high waters from snow melt,
From where it is small, the Little Big Horn,
I can hear a feeling of life, kind and gentle in your voice.
Here take my hand and roll in my arms for a choice
Premium touch of the feeling of life in love.
Think you can see the stars with me sometime?
The silent stars of the day smile invisible feelings
Left in time. In time, feelings will grow,
But you have to look in the direction of the mountain
As it is said, if you want to see me,

If you want to see me, I will be on the mountaintop,
The mountaintop where the mountain sheep are
Is where I will be. And so, if I am in your prayers
You possess the magic to create your feelings.

DAYTIME STAR

Blue, purple, pink under-stroked clouds
Were furious as they surrounded a dab
Of turquoise gold-dusted sky
Off below the Daytime Star
Alone in such beauty, he rode out
To drag the night lay over our Mother Earth.
The Daytime Star brings the feelings
To the heart, heading for tomorrow filled with love.
Every day you will be upon this ground forever,
Daytime Star.

IN THE HORSE SHEDDING MOON

To be in love
Is the greatest feeling
Upon sacred Mother Earth.
May you and yours get enough of
This beautiful feeling in your soul's being,
Deep in your hearts, this holy birth,
We want to stay for many winters.
May these married ones trust and respect
Each other for a good image to reflect
The way of life they lead where enters
A good lodge complete in good all around.
To hold hands and gaze into stars of dreams,
To awake into the eyes of the one you love beams
A heart that is good in love's sound.
Wishful thoughts and prayers are made for you
So enjoy a good life together, anew.

LISTEN

Love is a feeling that frequents the heart's emotion and soul,
You are the scent of love's flowers,
The beauty that draws feelings of love
With warmth touches the most sensuous
Of feelings I've longed in the wind
That rushes through the Wolf Teeth Mountains
I've the feeling that belongs in your heart,
I was lucky this morning in the soft pink twilight
The distinctly-featured points of Wolf Teeth
Overlapped the lower portion of the sky
Reminding me of how feelings moved in my heart
After looking into your eyes
I realized I finally made it to a tomorrow
That is filled with the scent of love's flowers,
Never really been out of my heart for so long
That I just want to lie out on the grass
Underneath the new crescent moon,
But this is only the moon after sun turned to summer,
Love is a feeling that frequents the heart's emotion and soul,
You are the scent of love's flowers
The beauty that draws feelings of love
Warm touch the most sensuous
Of feelings I've longed in the wind
That rushes through the Wolf Teeth Mountains
I've the feeling that belongs in your heart,
You are the feeling of love
That whispers through the pines
Of the Wolf Teeth Mountains
As the sun slowly slips over the Shot Boulder Mountains.
Yes, you are the fresh pure dew
Upon the newly born grasses and flowers
Barely enough for the horses to nip,

So listen to the wind tonight
Whisper the possibilities of a dream
That whispers through the pines of Wolf Teeth,
Have you listened to the wind?

THE FEELING THAT YOU ARE STILL

The feeling that you are still greets me in the morning
With the beautiful colors of pink and blue
I am a cowboy looking for horses in the pine whisper
    of feelings.
The ash trees are turning yellow and the plums
    turned last week.
We had frost last week, it flat killed the leaves on box elder
    trees up the creek.
I got the mares back a few weeks ago—short eight,
    so I have to keep on riding.
That is the part of life I love, throwing my saddle on the horse.
The dawn of a feeling that brings the beauty of the day
Arrives in the smoke of the many camp fires
    of the Minnakanjew
Dakota, Striped Arrows Cheyenne, Raven's Children Crow,
    Arapahoe, Shoshone,
There is no limit to love like the many stars in the sky, endless.
Last night a star softly whispered of how love starts a dream
    in the heart's reality,
Love quest appealing to the eye, thriving to appear
    as reflection in the eye
Of the one you want to love you, so you wait with her in view.
Then one day when the tribe is at the river to fetch water
A man and his son hide in the thick willows out of sight
As women pass on the sandy well-worn trail to the river
They would throw a clump of Mother Earth
    at the dream woman
To see her reaction, if she turned the whites of her eyes
    to see who is there,
Then she was not the one to make a life with, out on the trail
    of the buffalo.

When they find a good looking young woman walking
  with mother and grandmother,
Who would not turn to see where the clump of Mother Earth
  came from that hit her shoulder,
They would follow her to the water's edge
  and in front of the people on our side, tribe,
The love seeker would walk out into the twilight
  on the reflection of a lavender-colored river
To stand next to the reflection of the chosen dream woman
  to ask for a drink of water.
This was the beginning of courtship
  if there was to be in the heart of a beautiful woman.
The nod I do lends itself to the feeling of love that we reach for.

OVERLAP

Sun's shadow we'll never see,
Nor feel the warmth of a star's light
Riding above cloud shadows in fall gather,
Running bucking horses through timber
Gives sorrel blaze quite a lather.
Hope canyon's feelings I remember
Who radiated my plight as trite
A feeling marked a stray left to be,
Silky rose petal that melts in mouth
Reaching for you from the south,
A horse fell in love with a horse trader
Discursive days
After a vicious face-off with reality
Gave in to no feeling again
While naiad guards spring of love,
Love is a lasting, fleeting moment
In the feeling behind the reflection.
The fire dances
To any beat
Of the drum,
I glance,
Welcome, greet
For love's crumb.
You are the feeling
Of a flower in my heart
Among the wild grasses.
Love is set gently in the heart
In the beginning for a lifetime.
Reflections of life in the stars
Directions for us in the wind,
Days are filled with unwanted feelings
Night's sleepless wandering of useless thought,

Dull drums, blues with no origin
Grasp another feeling in time
To stare off into yonder motionless silence
Fixed on a feeling left behind, discarded
By one who wants no tomorrow.
He never returned from yesterday
When your memory reached out for a hold
Of his feelings to excite,
In the ground-appearing moon
Where snowflakes flew in sunlight,
Later full moon in apogee
Shows more color in the night,
Once in a blue moon
Your feeling comes by,
As an emotional barrier.
Saw her pony's tracks
Headed down the creek,
Lost tune of memory
Sing to me lyrics of love,
O lost tune of memory,
In search of a blue roan pony
Dancing in the shadows
Of a feeling in love,
And for love to look the other way
Is worse than dying today,
Lazy rhyme looks into haze
As a day of love betrays
The feeling it was intended for,
Fantasy blowing in from a past reality
Front of a twilight where smoke's feelings,
Shadows of souls cross, overlap in life.

ROSES FOR THE MATADOR

Roses for the matador
Plume for the buffalo bull

Parade of matadors
As they open the double doors,
Granite bullfighting ring in Madrid,
In feelings I keep under a lid,
Matadors step in time with marching song
Played by shiny brass horns,
Three handsome, elegant, elaborately dressed
Matadors showing their pride,
Displayed anticipation of test of courage and bravery.
Gold design decorated heavily down outside
Of white pant legs that ended at calf,
Bright bleached white socks with black slip-on shoes,
Short epaulet on shoulders firm
Over a short light jacket and red tie,
Years of training have brought them into this mighty arena
For a competition in the dance with death,
Each flanked by three understudy matadors.
The prancing horses of four heavily armored picadors
With the rest of the workers in plain white clothes, who follow.
Two mules in fancy decorated harnesses
Prance lively as if also showing their pride
Bring the end of the parade of matadors.
The skilled, poised matador calmly steps up
To greet the president, the power that is.
The arena is cleared and the stage is set.
Alone, the mighty matador walks out center,
Cheers and applause as the chute gate opens,
Sharp, pointed, wide-horned, black bull charges,
Head high searching to focus on matador,

Runs full blast to hit the matador
Who just lifts and swings his cape, bull on by.
A couple of passes, then his assistants
Step in to test the movement of the bull,
High energy softened by the picadors.
Again the understudies stick
Fancy decorated sticks into hump.
The mighty matador enters with his sword,
The bull passes by, gets closer and closer,
Under the matador's spell his horns go skyward.
Ola, ola, we cheer!
Permission granted for the kill,
The bull comes in straight,
Sword into heart to step aside
In the nick of time, horns brush
The matador in bull's last breath,
Dance with death, matador won today,
Red blood of bull connects to matador's tie.

Roses for the matador
Plume for the buffalo bull

On a flat top along the Stillwater
Toward where it is winter all of the time,
From the Bear Tooth Mountains,
A mighty buffalo bull is slowing toward death,
Many arrows are sticking out of his massive body,
Stands waiting to charge as he sticks his
Bloody tongue up his nostrils, waves his tail, straight up.
"Bring the little boy. Everything is set,"
Said Yellow Weasel as Deer Nose,
A little boy of ten winters, is brought
Out carrying an eagle plume tied to leather strap.
Howling Wolf runs by the wounded buffalo
To test his movement, the next time

Howling Wolf makes his pass, Deer Nose jumps on
The mighty buffalo bull from his tail
To tie the plume behind his horns,
Quickly jumping away from the horns of death.
A test of courage for men of the *Apsaalooke*
In the touch of death.
Songs are sung in praise of Deer Nose
As he walks toward becoming a man.

Roses for the matador
Plume for the buffalo bull

Deuwachishik, you I love.
Love of mother and father,
Of sister and brother,
Is the origin of love.
Love is origin of love,
Since before you arrived
From your nine moons stay
In the womb of your blood mother
Till moon ten onto Earth Mother.
Your life of love begins as reflection
Of horizon upon your water's affection,
Love lives in peace and contentment
For days on end.
Heart-felt moments I recall
Cheek to cheek, light
With a hug so tight
Each morning from Grandmother Everything She Joins.

Deuwachishik, you I love.
A silent nod of approval
And assurance of love
To walk out into a prayer,
Watch me always
With my people
I want to stay in good
For many winters to come.
My people, you know,
Where my blood is from,
On my father's side
On my mother's side,
Watch those people.
My Lodges of Driftwood parents, siblings, children
Remember them for me.

The people that I love,
The ones I love,
Watch them.
We don't want to use
Something of no origin,
Let our hearts be good
And all of us, let us love one another.

Deuwachishik, you I love.
The sun just set,
Thinking how we met,
Half moon out to fly
In the middle of the sky
Above cotton pink clouds,
Dreamt of your whereabouts
To wonder
What it is that you'd look like.
How would it feel
To feel so strong?
How would it feel
If I ever saw you?

The horizon upon waters of love's reflection
Where flow my feelings of affection,
I am from the tip of love.
The grasses were growing
And flowers were showing
When through a kiss
We entered softly into one another's souls.
Outrageous desires of mounts we rode
Into love free upon feeling told,
Of a heart that is good,
Alongside Chiron
Passions of thirst quenched
For peace was absolute.

MOUNTAIN WITH SOMETHING BEYOND

Top of Wolf Teeth, toward where it is cold all of the time,
From Mountain with Something Beyond
Looking into Cook Stove Basin for remnants of feelings.
It was a cold day after a skiff of hard crackling snow,
I was greeted by a cold shoulder of early winter wind
Lonesome, chilled to the bone, chasing cattle through timber
To finally lose them in the brushy thorn thickets.
Again trying to head a wild cow away from the brush,
She hit my horse a couple of times before entering thorns,
Too tight and fast for my rope today.
Three pairs of brush poppers I leave behind to
Get a couple headed home,
High calibration of events edged in silver and gold,
Beautiful feelings, remembrance from rodeo trail.
Left behind gates have been closed except for summer pasture,
Just the wild ones roaming the tops of Wolf Teeth.
You see? I ride this big rugged country alone
So I thank the Maker for watching me ride through the timber
And to go down and up these steep shale sides,
I say, *uhoe,* thank you,
This life is worth the wait from the Little Big Horn.
Anxious you are, my grandfather would say,
Everything is set. They knew you were coming.
Your scarf will watch you and your pony,
Go and ride.

MASS IN CROW

Last night I was out with my buffalo brothers
In songs and prayers,
Where colors swirled and sparkled.
To his death
Columbus thought he had discovered Asia.
Jesus was crucified
And Nixon saw impeachment.
Open pit mining left tailings bleached
To blast your sight.
They poisoned and polluted
The virgin pure waters.
Buffalo ate the grass,
Barbwire was in his stomach.
Birds use shredded threads of nylon tarps
Instead of horse hair for nests.
Farm boys who once cleared fields of rocks
Now make a trail of rocks in fields
For center-pivot irrigation system tires.

The moon and sun move around the teepee
As we smoke with the ground
And feed the water
In cosmic universal alliance walk.

Oedipus Rex, archway to the West,
The wolf dog barks and growls at the dark,
Polyphonic politician mumbles riddles,
But we dry the wild turnips and wild carrots
To walk toward another winter.
Mass is in Crow and Indian ceremonies in English
Self foe society fights for a better reclamation
Cattle now graze in sight of dragline.

As a better moon is rising
We recognize the person whispering to the horse.

The moon and sun move around the teepee
As we smoke with the ground
And feed the water
In cosmic universal alliance walk.

RIDE WITH ME

Ride with me beyond preexisting truths
  only accessible through the Valley of Thought.
In the Valley of the Chiefs, we the *Apsaalooke*
  have put together Little Big Horn College
Under the principle that a free nation must be governed
  by men free of ignorance,
That a real democracy in education
  shall provide an equal opportunity for the willing.
At one time, a long time ago, when silence was
  and was not a word,
There was nothing but air that is black,
  all in shadow, the dark night,
And since that time Old Man Coyote first used
The winds of thought among the stars.
We the *Apsaalooke* have entered the thoughts of life,
To say thought is how you become a real human being.
Itchik dau luom, it is good that you have come.
Wishful thoughts and prayers are how we are a people.
Upon the reflection of the sunrise's twilight
  on the waters of Higher Learning
May you be able to gently cup your hand
  for a beautiful life of intellect.
We are but a minute part of the universe
  asking to live in harmony
As we offer tobacco to our sacred Mother Earth.
To the Ones Who Listen in the four directions of the wind,
And to the Seven Stars, the Buffalo Bulls, we too want forever.
Western Civilization knew nothing of the Seven Seas,
The world was flat but Columbus thought otherwise
And to this end he thought he found a part of India.
Soon after the unknown was divided up in subsidies
The first Anglo sighting of an *Apsaalooke,* the Mountain People

split with the Hidatsa, about ten winters prior
To the Lewis and Clark encounter at the Three Forks
    of the Big River Missouri.
About twenty-three winters after horseshoes
    on the winter count and firewater in veins
The mountain men wanted the Friendship Treaty
    so all was well in peaceful waters.
Fort Laramie Treaty of 1851 established the *Apsaalooke* territory
    to be thirty-nine million acres
From the head of the Powder River
    to the head of the Yellowstone River
On over to the Judith Basin
    to complete the scratch on the ground
At the mouth of the Powder River where tomorrow is from.
Treaties were made and broken, under the statement:
*This treaty will stand as long as the grass grows
    and the river flows.*
Apsaalooke warriors were considered a sovereign nation
    on the plains and in the mountains.
The first Crow Indian student was the son of Wolf Bow, in 1870,
On Mission Creek about seven walks from where Elk River
    flows out from the *Apsaalooke* Mountain Range.
A few winters later smallpox blankets
    were given to the *Apsaalooke,* but we survived.
Any Indian off the reservation was considered a hostile
    and was to be shot on sight.
Kill the babies, too, for from the nits come the lice,
And the only good Indian is a dead Indian, so Custer had to die
On June 25, 1876 in the Valley of the Little Big Horn.
We have sent our young to be educated
    at Carlyle, Bond School, Flandreau, then on
To Lodge Grass School, Hardin High School,
    and Plenty Coups High School
To Haskell Institute, Bacone College,
    Montana State University—then, now.

HEART THIEF

The quest for the feeling of life
Spun into the magic twinkle
Of the beautiful woman
Who followed the flute music
Still walks in my heart.

The heart thief, drover of feelings,
Rode on over the ridge, down a draw,
Whipping over and under as he recklessly rides
To head off the horses that he has claimed,
His flames cannot be seen
As he deals with a mute pool of people.

RED SCARF

Boots and chinks
Silver bit and silver spurs
Eased into the dawn
To walk out kinks.
Horse shiny, free of burrs
Trotted into day,
I'm riding bay

If you can see the beauty
In the sunset with many colors,
I only see the beauty
In the sunrise with many colors.
You can find me
In the beauty in the sky,
In sunrise and sunset,
In the shadow of the sky
Among the stars.

If you can see the beauty in the sky
You can find me in your eye
With a red scarf on,
Boots and chinks.
Here I am, I'm riding gone,
Ground about day,
Looking for a stray,
Redtail hawk blessed me with his shadow,
Clouds peak to my south,
Granite to the west,
Sheep Mountains and the Pryors
Look their best
Grass full grown.

As I stood
In my heart that is good.

If you can see the beauty
In the sunset with many colors,
I only see the beauty
In the sunrise with many colors.
You can find me
In the beauty in the sky,
In sunrise and sunset,
In the shadow of the sky
In the shadow of the sky
Among the stars.

THE EVOLUTIONARY ALFONSO DELUPE

Just to see
The awe of the mountains
Is good enough,
A view of Crazy Mountains.
Just to be is good enough.
You see, this was
A free country
Before America ever was.
Under the laws
Of nature
The mountains, our Mother.
Then the other
Laws of man
To control the land
Through all this,
Don't miss
The laws of God
Twisted by man.
A viewer of Crazy Mountain
He came walking
From out of the past,
Born in the future,
A hundred years late,
Haunted memories talking.
Here, take a blast
In accepting
A foreign society
From a dying race,
Life left trace
Under the shadow of pollution
Hidden by the corruption
Of a plastic and

Chrome-plated society,
Wrote Alfonso Delupe, the evolutionary,
A flower child of the Sixties,
Freedom of love,
Social injustice never ends,
Who has not accepted
All of the pollution
Before the sunrise
As the people buyers arrived.
"Who me?" said the evolutionary,
"Yes, I work.
I work for Thoughts, Inc.
I'm the head dreamer
In the Feelings Department.
Sure, I'm responsible.
My responsibility is to the Earth.
The Earth, when she becomes nothing,
We, too, become nothing.
For you see,
My blood, this ground it is mixed with
Equal justice under law
Your veins belong, not to you
Queen Liz claimed 'em too."

HORIZON PEOPLE

People at the horizon
Where the sky and ground are one,
To there some people run.
They're nowhere, from nowhere they'll be gone.
They are neither in the sky or on the ground
For at the horizon
Where the sky and ground are one
White society they aren't,
Indian society they aren't,
For at the horizon
Where the sky and ground are one
There is nothing, all around
In the circle horizon, all around
Clothes blowing in the wind
Some people, that way they were.
Clothes blowing in the wind
When all the clothes
Can't help what you really are,
The Indian at the turn of the century,
The high plains centaur
In a tuxedo.
Some, their talk they forgot
For they were bought
To change their name
Just to play the game
As they ran to the horizon
To become clothes blowing in the wind.
The people at the horizon
Where the sky and ground are one . . .
Said my Grandfather Owns Painted Horse,
"Your talk, if you don't lose
And your lodge of Driftwood (clan)

If you always know
And have somewhere to run,
You will always be a child
Of the Large Beaked Bird, for winters many."
Our wishful thinking
What if thinking
What if thinking
To us
It was given—they say
Our praying
Along with it, was given to us—they say
These two, with them
People we are to become
Said my Grandfather,
They sell buck reins, don't they?
The same holds true today.

My heart inside
I still love you.
Last night
I dreamt, I saw you.
You, with me, traveled.
My heart was good
When your hand I held,
But then I traveled,
Awake from dream that's good.
Wild horse corralled
To jump into a feeling.
My heart inside,
I love you.
Seems you were here just yesterday,
Just a step in time,
Walking along the river,
Going upstream,
Starting to play the game.
Starting to play the game, again.
The cowboy . . .
With silver heart conchos

The cowboy
With silver heart conchos
Rides out
Into infinity
Singing,
What man was,
He still is.
For the smell of bison blood,
The taste of money,
Has been around

For eons.
The peak of life
Is still at the tip
Of the buffalo grass,
Even though
They've broken
The Sacred Circle,
Deteriorating ozone layer
Of Indian ecological thought.
I go on singing,
Paint horse, I will ride.
Painted sorrel,
That, I will ride.
Paint horse, I will ride.
Painted sorrel,
That, I will ride.

II

Reflections & Shadows

As crescent moons come and go
With each winter of snow
May you ride in beauty.

FAT ON RIBS

The tough winter weather will not leave,
The sun will not come out,
And I am out of hay.
The fat wore off the ribs
Of my riding ponies,
This is the toughest of winters.
Seems like there is no sign
Of my being out in feeling today,
For the drifts are getting high,
Need to get more crystal licks
And straw for hay.
Lost a calf to coyotes last night
And a cow died in the creek.
My father, Walks With The Wolf,
Prayed for the sun to come out,
That was yesterday,
And yesterday washed away.

MOON

The movement of the wind is held high
In the sky position of the moon
To foretell what the clouds bring for us.
The crescent returns she, apogee,
Turns to see grandchildren in movements
With the earth in shadows of teepee,
For rain or light snow to come by.
Granddad said cowboy too was in tune
With movements of the ground, movements of the moon.

All I've known is a lonely moon,
Among gathering birds and yellowing leaves
Was the feeling in my shadow
That stood out in a lonely moon,
Never really wanted this tune
That seems more severe in the eves.
Then, from nowhere, on the meadow
Happiness evolves from a loving moon,
But nineteen moons does Saturn have
To leave each love with a half,
Where half of half will never meet,
The perfect moon I'll never greet.
Lost in the random rise
Of love with no compromise
As many feelings and moons coincide,
After dawn vanishes in thin air,
A nightly feeling descends
Into lavender purple pink bottom clouds,
Reality slips out from the horizon,
Saddled up, riding alone
To scan the remains of the summer range
For signs of lost cattle,
Tracks of feelings in days we've past
Return in life, free to roam range,
In my humble horse grange,
The feelings of life around my saddle,
Locoweed-tainted shadow feeling cast
In sun turning lonely moon.

OMAHA REFLECTION

Sitting out here alone
With my feelings in the moon,
Let me whisper
A feeling in your ear
To touch your heart
With the feelings in the moon,
From feeling your beauty rose
To color feelings, transpose,
But until the shine
Returns to the ice
Through the sun,
Feelings set in time,
As morning arrives
I straddle the line-backed dun,
The black bird, raven,
Took away the wrong feeling
As drum beats slowly
On down through memories,
Horse tracks in mud
Smooth out in winter snow,
For the grass will grow
And feelings will flow
Over horse tracks in the mind,
I remembered a rainbow of feelings
That sparkled and flew out of my heart,
But horse tracks in the mind
Smooth out in rain and snow,
Feeling in buffalo grass remains
To lie in rosebud petals of dreams
Embedded in sweet sage and wild peppermint,
The scent of love is in the wind

From the Sierras to the Charles River,
Your feeling is in the moon,
I walk on the reflection of the moon.

OXBOW

To meet death filled with the hope
That life is made of love and dreams.
Is the war pony raring to go?
Spent love and dreams can no longer keep the lope
That the rest of life's remuda steams
Through their nostrils' rhythmic blow.
"Should have died
When I was stuck to a wild horse,"
An old man replied
At an oxbow to life's meandering coarse.
But then, he remembered Grandfather,
Remembering what the warriors would say,
"Before I have the toothache-bother,
Take me away to never see that day."
War paint from a dream was put on
And markings on horses were drawn
To meet death filled with the hope
That life is made of love and dreams.

The vines of thought that choke feelings
Rooted deep in the heart where time is unknown,
I was tangled among last night,
Death was banging on my wall
He was wanting me to go for it all.
He has been coming early
Or late at night, when I am alone,
Leaves me to think
Of where we would meet,
I've thought of how to say
Good-bye to everyone I've met,
In the midst of a battle
With a buffalo bull testicle-covered rattle,
A warrior stands singing
As whoops and hollers are ringing,
With rawhide around an ankle
He stakes himself to the ground,
The end is now for he no longer
Wants to handle the sacred fire of life
So he wants to give his body
Back to the water, ground and wind.
He drops his buffalo bull testicle-covered rattle,
Draws out his knife
As a warrior from Lodges That Are Different
Rides upon him fast to a skidding stop
Within the radius of the rawhide rope.
The death wish fight begins in the dust of hoofs.
When the dust settled he stood in the middle
Of four dead warriors from Lodges That Are Different.
He cuts the rawhide rope, jumps on his horse
To follow the pipe carrier chasing

The warriors from Lodges That Are Different,
"If it gets worse, I can always kill myself,"
Said the warrior who was spared.

Empty eyes,
This morning
When I awoke
Heard the birds chirp,
Blind to a feeling,
I rolled up my bed
To skip a flat rock
Over reality.

DURING THE NIGHT

During the night a creature wrapped around us
In the morning it died from our campfire.
When we crawled out, I told my brother
Not to eat the cooked meat
That smelled so good, although we were hungry.
When the day-time star appeared
My brother's arms and legs fused together as one,
His skin developed scales like a water being,
For he ate the cooked meat from the creature.
I set my brother into the deep still water as he said,
"Feed me pounded dry meat when the moon appears."
In the ground-appearing moon,
I fed the water and my brothers and sisters,
The water beings, who watch us human beings.
The Children of the Large Beaked Bird say,
"Water, I feed you, whatever is in the water,
My brothers and sisters, watch me always
And let me return to my lodge at night fall."

One time, a long time ago,
A little boy was out gathering ghost tobacco.
When he returned to camp
In the afternoon, one of the Ones Without a Body,
A ghost, entered the camp and said,
"Doemuxdaydum duksdee."
The people all scattered and ran.
Even to this day no one knows
What it is that the ghost said.
The little boy was told
To never touch the ghost tobacco again.
People who know nothing
Think that everyone should think as they do.

EYES TAKE OUT

Clouds lift up Ruby Valley
As the medicine man unveils
Feelings of illusion.
The poet paints with wails
Of inner heart commotion,
Life is a song of feelings.

Long ago, in a far-away land
Lived a cowboy on a forgotten creek
Out of reach of reality,
He saddles up to a fantasy
As he rides on feelings in the wind,
A red roan longhorn bull sang him a song.

The maker of the horse was Poseidon
For the ones who believe the words
Of Achilles' mistress, Hippodamia Briseis.
Hercules' mount, Arion, came from the tapping
Of Neptune's trident upon the ground,
It's right hooves were that of a human,
Powers from the God of the Sea to talk,
Achilles' Balios: Sire the West Wind,
Dam Swift Foot, a Harpy,
Skienfauxi is the Norse horse of the day,
Alsvid is the chariot horse of the moon.
Virgil says Ericthonious was first to have four in hand,
The night's horse is Hrimefaxi (Xreemaufauxi),
A frost mane that showered the earth
With frost that flew from its bit,
Roman Emporer Caligula's mount, Incitatus,
Was considered a priest and consul,
Drank wine from a golden pail in an ivory manger,
Odin's eight-hooved gray horse, Sleipnir,
Is from the eight points of the wind,
It could travel on land and sea,
Muemosyne, the Goddess of Memory,
Daughter of Heaven and Earth,
I've asked of the horse's story, and that was it.
This woman, a Child of the Large Beaked Bird,
Was purified in bear root smoke,
With the heat and prayers of a sweat lodge,
Here fingernails and toenails were cleaned,
And she was rubbed with sweet sage
In her preparation to fast on an island,
On the fourth morning
When all of her human smell was gone,

She heard a sound she had never heard before,
In the time when buffalo jumps,
Songs lured buffalo over a hidden cliff,
The whinnying of horses
Mixed with the sound of splashing water
At the island's edge,
In the morning sun horses emerged
From the water's pure white foam.
The Spirit Being said, "This creature is the horse.
Take him to your people to carry the load
That the wolf-dog is now carrying.
With him, you can ride up to the buffalo,
Your people's lives will become easier.
Don't strike him in the face for horses have a soul,
And they talk with each other.
This creature, the horse, is a gift from the water.
Take good care of them."

RIVERS OF HORSE

All you real human beings, listen.
This is the story of the coming of the horse.
The Spanish barb the Comanche rode,
The mystic pony the Shoshone stole,
Drifting up from the Rio Grande
To the Columbia River Basin,
Mighty herds the Cayuse drove,
Mighty herds of horses.
Out of a dream they came to the Crow,
Sioux, Cheyenne and Arapaho,
Through the Northern Plains and mountains grazed,
Around the wolf and buffalo strayed,
Flowing herds of horses,
Rich flowing herds of horses.
Rivers of horse,
Rich rivers of horse,
Up and down these coulees and draws,
From the Rio Grande, the Platte
And the Powder River, flow herds,
Of this mystic pony,
Of this mystic pony.
Tapping willow stick, I can still hear,
I can still hear my grandfather
Tapping painted black with a willow stick.
At one time, a long time ago,
My Grandfather Owns Painted Horse
Behind him I sat
On his horse painted black,
I hugged him lightly
As I leaned the right side of my face
Gently against his back,

These horses have a soul,
Do them good and respect them.
Talk good to them and they know.
They talk to each other, they say.
"When you talk good to the horse's spirit,
They will come to you, and you will be
Lucky with them in a heart that is good,"
Said my Grandfather Owns Painted Horse.
At the edge of my eye something went by,
It returned into my feeling,
You're so far away from me
As I stare into the twinkle and glitter
Of blowing snow flakes in the wind.
Before, the warrior was respected,
The hides on his lodge reflected
The quality of horses he rode,
Great horses made great warriors,
Atop a fast running buffalo horse
He could catch a fast running buffalo,
To stick an arrow behind the last rib
And deep into the heart.
The warrior's people ate the best of meat
Packed on his many horses.
The war horse was the most prized of steeds
Tied to his thigh as it grazed outside
The lodge by night. This was the war horse,
He used to strike the grand coup
As he ran up on the enemy to touch him
While he was still alive,
Many feathers of grand coup,
And return with many horses
Make for a long-tailed war bonnet.
Great horses made great warriors.
The second best coup
Was to enter the enemy camp by night,

To cut the rawhide rope attached
To the sleeping enemy warrior's top mount.
From a dream he was given this
White sorrel medicine horse paint
In the shadow of Shining Mountains,
In the moon of the first thunder,
Atop his medicine horse paint, he could
Swoop up a beautiful woman to steal
From Lodges That Are Different from his.
His song they would sing
As he danced the scalp dance and the victory dance,
To give away the best of horses,
Fast running horses, to spread
Good fortune among his people,
He was close to the horse's spirit,
On the great war horse
He could kill the enemy,
Lead a successful war party,
To become the chief, the man that is good.
The Maker blessed him with great horses,
So he had someone to lean his back against.
The great horse made the warrior great.
Remembered pulling strands of sinew thread
To run through my mouth, to pinch one end,
Then to roll-twist the rest down the outside
Of my right thigh, on late snowy winter night.
I got up to poke the fire,
When Grandmother Everything She Joins
Recalled this story:
"A horse that is good,
Their brother-in-law they would give
To show love and respect for their sister.
A girl's parents would give
Ten good horses to a great warrior
To marry their daughter.

But a man who is not a man
Would give horses to a girl's parents
For the girl's hand in marriage,
So the great warrior would have
Many horses and many wives.
Back when the woman lived with the man,
Before, that's how it was.
The children of a respectable family
Would ride Appaloosa horses
With no tails as a prestige symbol,
The rest of the old folk's horses,
And children's horses wore squared-off tails,
These great horses made people great
Out in the northern mountains and Plains,
Where horses and women were stolen
In intertribal Plains warfare.
Bird Horse, Horse On The Other Side,
Medicine Tail, Pretty Paint, Rides the Horse,
Takes the Horse, Horse Herder, Spotted Horse,
Brings Home Many Geldings, Has a Lot of Colts,
Lucky with His Horse, Always Rides Horses,
Gray Horse Rider, Sorrel Horse, Buckskin Horse,
Black Horse Rider, Lead Horse Rider:
These are our names from a horse culture.
Then, there was a day when all of my father's horses
Were killed by the Bureau of Indian Affairs,
And Sell Out Indians for twenty-five cents an ear.
So too with the coyote and magpie,
But they survived in time,
Before that, the buffalo and wolf were gone.
After this, the sheep and spotted buffalo
Were brought in to eat the buffalo grass,
"Don't shed a tear for the horses
For they replace a human being's life,"
Said my Grandmother Everything She Joins,

Florence Medicine Tail Real Bird,
"But that day, I made my tears drop
When they killed all the horses.
That day was bad, my heart was bad.
If these were days like those when lodges used to move,
My heart would be extremely good."
Painted Black Horse Rider, Spirit Horse Rider,
Protector and Defender of the Crow
Who still rides the prairies and mountains,
I have always been told about you.
So now I offer you Painted Black Horse Rider,
My sacred pipe for many good tomorrows.

NEW INDIAN SONNET

We are a minute part of an order in the universe
Where the heavenly waters bless the buffalo grass
And life through time immemorial can continent transverse,
Not for us to disrupt integral balance in food chain mass,
Revengeful proposition for mute opposition in nature's wonder,
Bison domino Indian, wolf and horse repercussion
Inhuman behavior in Washington board room ponder,
Buffalo Bill overshadows Custer's failure on reservation
After winters many, again we've reached this point,
This time the cowboy is the new Indian of the west,
Money sails again in breeze as lawmakers anoint
The wolf to set the cowboy in the Indian's nest,
We walked on moon and brought fire in house,
Possess thoughts in a mind where life and death are spouse.

ALCOHOL FETAL SYNDROME

Many, many moons and winters of oppression
Piled on top of misunderstandings permeated
Three to four generations of inhalants,
Glue, paint, gas, disinfectants,
Beer, wine, whiskey jitters,
Buzzing off walls, over and under desks, tables,
Such is the world where I teach and live.
Mood altering drugs have penetrated
The body, mind, the soul of Native Man.
One of my people gave birth to a baby
With cirrhosis who lived for seven moons,
A place where plain water is no longer blessed
And dreams from He Who First Did Everything
Are no longer seen, or honored.
In a world of chemicals, herbs, berries, grains,
Juices, chunks, powder and smoke, Native Man's
Aromas are from the fumes of feces and puke.
In the pungent smell of an herb
Or the firewater of your choice,
Independence through neglect, the lost Indians
Mill around awaiting their fate
For destiny is written in a date
That only demons in the Wolf Witcher Tobacco
Can control in the nightmares and cold sweats
That don't seem real to a credit-card-paying Pilgrim.
Anti-abortion and anti-corporal punishment believers
Should see this world in which I live
Where fear and respect do not exist.

He was never born,
They just found him next to a Lysol can,
And it is said

That his mother almost died of cirrhosis last winter,
But in the meantime
He is rolling a joint in the bathroom.

Minced words are soy meat philosophies,
Rasta-pasta colors fly in Rez atrocities,
Incestual genocide is a synthetic fog
Through a heavy mood altering drug bog,
After cavalry failed, but fifty winters later
Young Indian girls sterilization program favor,
Re-instigated before the 2nd World War,
So illegal drinker and non-voter Native soldier
Marries young sweetheart neutered
By a country he shielded himself for
Among the scattering of German bullets,
He was already dead, but returned.
There are not very many Indians left,
The official Indian is an enrolled member
Of a federally recognized tribe,
One quarter degree of Indian blood,
This is the legal Indian.
Residues of the Indian are descendants
Who exchange food stamps and eat comods.
Meaningless sounds of thought don't even exist
In their world of scores, the Egyptian ibis-
Marked medicine horse, they'll never know
For they lost the language of an unknown life.

The winos were huddled up at the bar's door
To get out of the wind, a lifetime blew past,
On the other side, some are lost in legal tender,
A restless soul walks up to the rainbow
Through the illusion of the Indian,
And says, "When you dream, and they talk English
In your dream, you are no longer an Indian."

CONSTELLATION

Run down mobile home trailers
Surrounded by broken down junkers,
White, clear and orange plastic jugs clutter us,
Reservation life skewed toward poverty
In a flimsy prefab, double wide world.
We cannot afford gas price increases,
Yet we are targets of federal funds
The remnants of old wool blankets
Of by-gone buffalo days,
Goals and objectives in our name yield money,
Doesn't make a Confederate dollar's worth of difference,
We are a revolving platter for everyone to swipe
While we marinate in alcohol, depression and laziness.
Aesthetic appearance of suicide is a shining star
While some hold books of blank pages.
They say we don't look like where we originated
Like beer advertisements that don't look like real drinkers,
Life in the tourist brochure so far reaching
That doesn't look like Indians in a homeless shelter.
We search for a maximum internal coherence
To get to the closest possible fit to nature,
For the new image of life in a healthy constellation.

NEAR FULL MOON

Today I saw the near full moon
The day-time star emerged, side by side,
Shortly after the sun took away the pink and blue
As I was riding home in front of a soft gentle night,
In this moon of ice on the teepees,
When an insecure Indian in a shaky voice
Read meeting minutes, it took me back in time
To that unsure stage of my bilingualism,
The hitchhiker's sign read, *Anywhere but here,*
And when I rode through the pines
They were drenched in heavy dew.
This is what I asked for from Grandmother Moon
When she showed us her moisture rings,
Rainbow rouge announced blurred ground
Among the fog and close to He Who First Did Everything.
My heart is good as I ride through these pines
When they are drinking water from above,
The most sacred of all the waters upon Mother Earth
Which bless my horse and me as I think of you.
Last night the moonlight was like day,
When I saw a feeling headed my way, then stopped.

It is the same wind that blew through the pines
When Sacagawea led Lewis and Clark up the Big River,
The Missouri River,
When my people greeted them on the Three Forks.
Now, two hundred winters later, I welcome you all.
Today as I look around,
It is the same wind that blows through the pines,
It's the wind that blows the same rush whisper
    through pine trees.
Welcome soft pink twilight of beautiful great day,
Upon the new snow lay unforeseen thoughts, they stay.
Sacagawea leads creed never seen before, tide low,
Explore rivers, high time Lewis and Clark might see
The mountain man's straight knife, Texas cowboys be free
Attitude now strikes pain, poison hard tack lace grain
Small pox blankets rage plight, Little Big Horn life strain,
Smooth it over treaty, rivers and grasses flow and grow,
The sod busters wave white and moving camp, no buy,
Headwaters, a mean life, kind and gentle tall soul,
It's the wind that blows, same clash of cultures ride by,
Rush, whisper through pine trees, it's the wind that blows same,
Timber wind that blows same, two hundred years sky break,
Buffalo wind blows same tune, coyote tracks reach blame,
Shooting star wind blows same, Butte's Acid White Lake,
Our Mother Earth polluted, sickness upon time fly
Asbestos deed drive-by, some hear call of society
Now good grass, wildlife graze, coal mine
Reclamation rate stout statute, rush whisper
through pine trees

Let us disarm discrimination but in reality do
Reconstruct our voting districts to get our horse to win
While the buffalo stray and wolf hunger,
Recapitulation of the pain-based food chain,
Let's make the application easier for the farmers,
There was never peace on the mountains and plains,
And up the Big River, where we are so small
    in the colorful sunrise
It is the same wind that blows thought through the pines.

Today I hear the snow that squeaks
From under my horse's feet,
Strong haze among the peaks
Of the mighty, cold Wolf Teeth
Bundles my thoughts of love for you,
As the sky weakly turns blue,
I ride slowly up Yellow Leggins
To look for horses to fill my count,
The beauty of Valley of Chiefs sparkles in the morning frost
Upon the snow of the Wolf Teeth
Over wind swept tips of emotion
That protrude from my heart as I ride up Yellow Leggins.
Last night I saw a dream. In that dream
I watched a war dance where they sang the Flag Song,
"You are a man that is good, your flag you've raised."
I want to see that day with you, so if you think of me
I will be among the Wolf Teeth Mountains.

III

Place Setting For A Feast Of People
No Longer Here

The promise of love and life in the moon
Beckons our rider to cinch real loose
For an easy day of riding through Yellowstone.
The mountain woman of Pueblo
Wore a pair of elk teeth
For the feeling that she is.
The beautiful Woman-of-the-Mountain
Told our rider to meet her on the Wind River
In the moon when the birds return.
Early morning's empty streets
Haunt as do late night road crosses,
All I can remember today are the losses.
Alone, traveling to celebrate winter's end,
People routinely work and wish for better.
He was a tarnished sun that rose
Rendering all of the reflection's pose.
Then I remembered myself, as feeling in wind,
The vision of a feeling drives the heart
Slowly through a life where people hide
From themselves in thick underbrush,
In the shadows of their hearts.
I want nothing to cling to your heart
As you go riding in life.
That is what I have asked for you.

ACROSS MONTANA ON HORSEBACK, POET HANDS OUT POETRY

. . . as heard on NPR's All Things Considered, *30 July 2010*

MICHELE NORRIS, host: If you're the Poet Laureate of the state of Montana, you could carry out your duties several ways. You could spend a lot of time talking to school children or promote poetry through the local libraries, perhaps talk to civic organizations.

Well, Henry Real Bird decided to get on horseback at one end of the state and ride halfway to the other, handing out books of poetry along the way. And we caught up with Mr. Real Bird as he's been doing just that. Exactly where are you right now?

Mr. HENRY REAL BIRD, Poet Laureate of Montana: I'm in Havre, Montana, along the Milk River. Tomorrow, I saddle up, and I drift off into the Bear Paw Mountains, and I end up over in Rocky Boy, Montana, my final destination.

NORRIS: Who are you traveling with?

Mr. REAL BIRD: I'm riding with my Hidatsa brother, Levi Bruce from Berthold Indian Reservation. As a Crow Indian, I'm a Hidatsa. Hidatsa and Crow were one tribe, and so our language is still . . . the grammar is still the same, and it's still pretty close. Like he says *biri* for water, and I say *bili*.

NORRIS: Could you do me a favor? We always hear about those big skies of Montana. What's that sky look like today?

Mr. REAL BIRD: It's so big that you can't really put an edge to it. That's how it is today in a vast sea of buffalo grass.

NORRIS: Henry Real Bird, tell me about the books that you're handing out and the reception that you get.

Mr. REAL BIRD: Oh, the books that I'm handing out are my books of poetry. I surprise some people, like at a café in Nashua, a guy that, he had two boys there, young boys, high school boys, I mean, just so much promise and so much future. And I just gave them the books so they can read that poetry.

That, plus once I give them out and other people, they see me coming out on horseback and they walk over and they say: *Where's my book?* And I just hand them a book from atop the horse and everything. And so I just want them to think, to move along in thought.

NORRIS: To move along in thought. That sounds wonderful. Now when they open up the pages of that book, could you just give us a small sample of what they would find? Would you mind reciting just a small bit of your poetry?

Mr. REAL BIRD: Oh, a little bit of it, okay.

"Sunrise Whirls": Recapitulation of sunrise whirls, thoughts of man, / Civilization recedes, waves on shore of sand, / Attached to a reality now touches in life's span, / Matched links mark beginning of end strand, / Scratched thoughts drawn on rock of cave preserve / Our humble beginning, recorded in computer reserve. / We question, wonder, learn origin and beyond, / Shifting winds up the canyon walls, no barrier. We yawn / From the constant vigil of progress that marches / Toward both ends of the spectrum cloning to nuclear arches. / We give life and take life.

NORRIS: You say we question, wonder and learn. I wonder what you're leaning as you travel across the state and travel across some of the parts of the state where your ancestors lived.

Mr. REAL BIRD: Yeah, I can see life itself out here in Montana on a trail of the buffalo that now goes between elevators going to Cirrhosis Park. And all of the drinking that is on the Indian reservation that I don't want to see, but I do because that is life, and yet I wait for coffee at the convenience store at Fort Belknap, and all of the workers—they're going to work for the day.

And so to be able to see the young families full of promise and hope and then to go along and to pick up words like 'Fur Cap Mountain.' That's the Indian word for the Little Rocky Mountains.

To be given all of these things, I mean people come by, and they feed me dry meat, bannock bread. They crush choke cherries and give them to me. It's a beautiful place when people come, and they hug you, and they bless you to continue on and asking for a safe journey.

NORRIS: Well, safe journeys to you. It's been a pleasure to talk to you. All the best.

Mr. REAL BIRD: Okay, may you ride in beauty, too, covered with love for many winters to come. *Uhoe,* we'll see you.

NORRIS: That's Henry Real Bird, cowboy, member of the Crow Nation and Poet Laureate of the state of Montana.

RIDE ACROSS MONTANA
WITH HENRY REAL BIRD

....

Transcript of interview with Henry Real Bird,
Western Folklife Center

RIDE ACROSS MONTANA
WITH HENRY REAL BIRD, JULY 21, 2010

HENRY REAL BIRD—cowboy poet, Crow Indian and recently named Poet Laureate of Montana—has embarked on a 415 mile journey on horseback across northwest North Dakota and northern Montana. He is handing out books of poetry to the people he meets along his route, which will take him through Indian country where his grandfather rode a century ago. This is not a press stunt, but rather a demonstration of Henry's life, culture and poetry: a journey of horse and horseman slowly making their way across a vast ancestral landscape.

HAL CANNON: Where are you Henry?

HENRY REAL BIRD: I'm over here along the Missouri River. I been ridin' here since Tuesday . . . so I've been on the road about 9 days. And I stayed last night at a town called Fraser.

HAL CANNON: Are you on a horse right now?

HENRY REAL BIRD: Yeah, I'm riding a horse right now along Highway 2 in Montana. What they call High Line.

HAL CANNON: Can you describe what you're looking at right now?

HENRY REAL BIRD: Oh gosh, just a vast amount of land . . . just rolling hills all over to the north, and then on over to the south I've got cottonwood trees in the valley floor of the Missouri River, north of the river. Then across the Missouri to the south we've got them hills there . . . the breaks . . . just beautiful.

HAL CANNON: Henry, I'm hearing cars just speeding past you. What's the difference between the way you're seeing what's going on and people going sixty miles an hour?

HENRY REAL BIRD: Oh yeah. The slow pace . . . you see more. I saw hills and creeks that I didn't know existed. I mean I've been on this road before but I never paid attention to it but now you see all this beautiful landscape. And uh . . . I mean this is good traveling here.

HAL CANNON: So where did you start out Henry?

HENRY REAL BIRD: I started out from the Fort Berthold Indian Reservation. We started out along the Missouri there on the trail of the buffalo, and uh, going through patches of sweet sage, eating Juneberries. And I was saying that life cannot get any sweeter than this. To be able to ride a horse for the day and then just eat the Juneberries. And when I got over here yesterday, they stopped me on the road and took me over and gave me some Juneberry pie. And I had some more again last night and I went over to the sweat lodge over here in Frazer, and prayed. They say the sweat lodge . . . you use that to remember who you are. But the whole thing is . . . places where my great grandfather rode over on Fort Berthold and over to Fort Union and then I just wanted to ride a horse right where they rode horses too, along the Missouri. And that's what I'm doing, and then giving out books of poetry along the way.

HAL CANNON: What is the reaction when you hand someone a book of poems?

HENRY REAL BIRD: They're surprised and they just browse through it right there, and they don't know what to think and so I'm gone by the next day so I don't know what they think. I just put my name on there and everything else. I just want them to enjoy the thought . . . enjoy the thought and go for the ride into the feeling whatever it is.

HAL CANNON: You were made Poet Laureate of Montana, is this part of what you think your job is as Poet Laureate for the state?

HENRY REAL BIRD: You know I took it on like that, because nobody else will ever do this type of thing, you know. Nobody has the guts to just saddle up a horse and just go from town to town just giving out books of poetry and stuff like that. And so I figure that I'm not like everybody else and that's why I'm the way I am, and so this is just my style of giving back to the people what I have taken from life out here in Montana.

HAL CANNON: Henry, I admire you.

HENRY REAL BIRD: Oh, I don't know it's just, uh . . .

HAL CANNON: I do, I count you as a good friend. I really appreciate what you do.

HENRY REAL BIRD: I appreciate you too because you've kept me alive. In the beginning when I didn't want to live any more, you guys kept me alive and that was alright, you know. And so I feel good today.

HAL CANNON: You've helped us. You've helped keep us alive my friend. So can we call you along the route and ask you how things are going?

HENRY REAL BIRD: Yeah, call anytime and wherever I am on the road if I get good reception we can connect.

HAL CANNON: Good luck on your journey and we'll call you in a few days.

HENRY REAL BIRD: OK. See you later then, OK. Bye.

HAL CANNON: Bye Henry.

. . . .

BIG SKY BIRTHDAY, JULY 24, 2010

IN THE SECOND of our series of conversations with Montana Poet Laureate Henry Real Bird, Western Folklife Center Producer Taki Telonidis called to wish him Happy Birthday and found him in the town of Malta near the banks of the Milk River. Henry has been on the road for nearly two weeks, retracing the travels of his ancestors and giving out books of poetry to people he meets in rural towns and Indian reservations along the way.

TAKI TELONIDIS: A couple of days ago you said you were doing this ride in part so you could ride horses like your grandfather and great grandfather did . . . in the same places. And I'm wondering as you're doing this, what sort of things are you thinking about? Is your mind taking you back to those days of your grandparents?

HENRY REAL BIRD: Back to those days. Like you get the feeling . . . not that you have been there before . . . but to know that your blood has been there two generations before you. Unbelievable! It makes you . . . it just makes you . . . you're so happy you just want to cry sometimes, just because you're so happy, you know.

TAKI TELONIDIS: That's beautiful. I'll bet you some poems will come out of this experience.

HENRY REAL BIRD: Oh no. I'm doing that, I'm doing that. In fact, I'm writing as I go along . . . in my mind I'm putting it all together. And then in the end I'm going to regroup and finish this thing off maybe in one poem. I don't know what I'm going to do. But I see awful things too . . . good things and bad things. Just like over in Wolf Point, Montana, I saw a lot of alcoholism there. So that was a depressing sight, but that is there. So I'll write a little piece in there to show that. Oh I've been wanting to use this line which I haven't been able to use: what have you done to life, or what has life done to you? And then to wander around like that. I've had that line painted on my heart for a long time and I haven't been able to really use it, but I'm going to use it there I think. I'm just working it all out.

TAKI TELONIDIS: One last question for you Henry. Today is your birthday and you're spending it on the banks of the Milk River and you're sixty-two now which I think entitles you to reduced admission to National Parks and all sorts of privileges. But does it also make you an elder? Do you consider yourself an elder?

HENRY REAL BIRD: Oh, I'm lucky to be an elder, and I appreciate that because of all the things that I have been though, and I'm lucky to be alive and I know that. And I appreciate that. You know they have that saying to where . . . long, long on the tooth or something like that . . .

TAKI TELONIDIS: Long in the tooth.

HENRY REAL BIRD: Yeah, long in the tooth, but for us they say when your eye tooth crumbles and your hair is pure white, nobody can outfox you. Nobody can outdo you in thinking. And so, for knowledge to turn into wisdom type of thing. I'm nearing that stage in life, type of thing. That's how we see it, yeah.

TAKI TELONIDIS: Henry, thank you very much. It's great to talk with you again, and we'll touch base with you in a couple of days.

HENRY REAL BIRD: Oh yeah, the next couple of days . . . tomorrow I'm going to stay over in Dodson, and then I'm going to finish off the fair there. So I'll watch the demolition derby there, then after that I'll be into Fort Belknap, and from then on I still have to make arrangements for the other end. But everything just falls into place. You just sort of kick your horse into the day and keep on going, and you run into something nice.

TAKI TELONIDIS: And the demolition derby sounds like it'll be a highlight.

HENRY REAL BIRD: *(laughs)* Oh God, yeah, yeah. I'm going to watch the demolition derby. I saw a poster here, so I'll be there for that. And I called ahead over there and they're going to let me stay over at the fairgrounds. So I'll have stables and everything for the horses, and no motel or anything . . . so I'll put up my tent and slowly drift out into the stars, you know.

TAKI TELONIDIS: Henry, it sounds great.

HENRY REAL BIRD: Good night.

TAKI TELONIDIS: Nice to talk to you.

HENRY REAL BIRD: Yeah.

POET HENRY REAL BIRD RIDES THE LAST STANZA OF HIS TREK ACROSS MONTANA, JULY 30, 2010

AFTER RIDING HORSEBACK for more than 390 miles over the past two weeks, our friend Henry Real Bird is one day's ride from his final destination at the Rocky Boy's Indian Reservation. Henry is the Poet Laureate of Montana, and he has traversed the state, visiting small towns and Indian Reservations along his route, distributing books of poetry. In this last installment of our conversations with Henry, he explains how this odyssey has given him a new perspective of his homeland, and of America.

HAL CANNON: What's the contrast of your pace and the people that are passing you by on the highway.

HENRY REAL BIRD: Yeah, I just saddle up and I go the pace of my horse, that's what I take care of. In the morning when its cool, I try to trot as much as I can to cover as much country as I can. When it heats up, I slow down and take a break. The movement of the horse, and the movement of Mother Earth, and the crescent moon we just came from. That's when I started out, at the crescent moon, on the Missouri River, and the Juneberries were just plentiful . . . to just be eating that when everybody is using the Blackberry or using the phone in an air conditioned RV, pulling a small vehicle, just cruising down the road. That's their style and that's good. But me, I just wanted to go back and be able to go slowly, and to meet the people and to see the land, yeah.

HAL CANNON: How many miles have you gone?

HENRY REAL BIRD: I think I've gone 395 miles, somewhere around there . . . because they said Rocky Boy is about 20 miles away.

HAL CANNON: So what's next for you, Henry?

HENRY REAL BIRD: After I do this one here, three hundred of my children's books are being shipped out and I pick them up and I distribute them at a youth rodeo at Rocky Boy, yeah. So that's what I'll be doing Monday or Tuesday.

HAL CANNON: You're busy . . .

HENRY REAL BIRD: Oh yeah, I'm lucky. I'm thankful that I'm able to do this. That type of activity that creates the exhaustion to where we can sleep good at night. I've had some good dreams. I saw a dream of snow flying a few days ago. I say that dream to all the people in radioland to where they will reach that day where the first snow fall is, and to be with their loved ones and to go through many of those first snowfalls upon sacred Mother Earth. And so I was able to be given that dream on the road here, and I enjoy that.

HAL CANNON: Henry, how was the demolition derby, by the way?

HENRY REAL BIRD: The demolition derby was the best. I haven't seen that since I was a little boy on Crow Agency. On this one here, they changed the rules and they have heats, but back in those days they'd get the infield of the race track and it's a free for all to the last car standing. But here they have rules and everything else. But it was good. . . . I mean those young families there, beautiful. Women and men with beautiful kids, and so full of promise. It just made you so happy to know that America is so beautiful, so full of dreams. And to put on the best clothes that they have to come out to the Fair reminded me of being young. Walking in new boots and new pants, going to the Billings Fair, the Montana State Fair. I was able to take in everything there. It was beautiful.

HAL CANNON: Henry, thank you very much for letting us be part of your journey and recording this. People have really enjoyed hearing your voice on our blog. It's really wonderful to be part of it.

HENRY REAL BIRD: I'm having a beautiful time.

HAL CANNON: Thanks, we'll talk to you soon. Let us know how it turns out.

Transcript of the interview with Henry Real Bird courtesy of the Western Folklife Center. This interview can be heard at: *http://westernfolklifecenter. wordpress.com/2010/07/23/ride-across-montana-with-henry-real-bird/*